NEON BABY

NEON BABY

NEON BABY

New and Selected Poems

AIDAN MURPHY

**NEW
ISLAND**

NEON BABY

First published 2007

by New Island

2 Brookside

Dundrum Road

Dublin 14

www.newisland.ie

ISBN 978-1-905494-59-0

British Library Cataloguing Data. A CIP catalogue record for this
book is available from the British Library.

Book design by Inka Hagen

Printed in the UK by Athenaeum Press Ltd., Gateshead, Tyne & Wear

New Island received financial assistance from

The Arts Council (An Chomhairle Ealaíon), Dublin, Ireland.

10 9 8 7 6 5 4 3 2 1

Contents

From *The Restless Factor* (1985)

From *The Way the Money Goes* (1987)

From *Small Sky, Big Change* (1989)

From *Stark Naked Blues* (1997)

From *Looking in at Eden* (2001)

Acknowledgments

Acknowledgments are made to the editors of the following publications in which certain poems first appeared:
Ambit; *Aquarius*; *Bananas*; *Cyphers*; Writing in the West (*The Connacht Tribune*); *Green Lines*; *The Green River Review* (USA); *Iron*; New Irish Writing (*The Irish Press*); *The Sunday Tribune*; *Omens*; *Poetry Ireland*; *Profiles 2* (The Profile Press, Dublin); *Quarryman*; *Tuba*; *Siting Fires*; *The Cork Review*; *Threshold*; *The Echo Room*; *North*; *Poetry Now*; *Rubicon* (Canada); *The Faber Book of Movie Verse*; *Volume* (Crawford Municipal Art Gallery, Cork); *The Shop*; *Poetry Readings at Bewley's 1989* (Fiona Burns, National College of Art and Design, Dublin); *Dog*; *Southword*; *Soho Square 6* (ed. Colm Tóibín); *Chameleons*; *The Stony Thursday Book*.

Introduction: Three Cities

In 1970, on the surface of things, I was safe and settled. After a couple of painfully misjudged but mercifully short-lived jobs – timekeeper on a building site, cost clerk in the motor trade – I successfully applied for the modest position of copyholder in the reading room of the *Cork Examiner*, then considered one of the most secure employers in the city. The wages were excellent, the night shifts suited me, and the prospects for climbing the ranks were wide open. I was 18 years of age with a guaranteed future in my hands.

But as a candidate for settling down and adjusting to reality I was a dead loss, a hopeless case. I had always been a bit of a faraway kid given to intense thousand-yard stares and lengthy daydreaming silences. I could observe a night sky for hours on end, sit on a shoreline oblivious to everything except the tide's ebb and flow, or lose myself so completely in a book that nothing would rouse me. Also, from mother's knee to a seat of my own, I had spent so much of my childhood in the picture-houses of Cork, sponging up visions of Hollywood light, that I was more familiar and comfortable with actors and their big screen dramas than I ever was with real people and real situations.

In those days of no options Cork was a sleepy hollow. Drab and poor, it cranked itself forward from day to day with a dull, solemn rhythm, profoundly and defensively ritualistic. Every day I saw the same faces, made the same small talk, but deep down I felt like an impostor. Since the mid-years of secondary school I'd been tormented by a desire that wouldn't take no for an answer: a desire to write. Worse than that, a desire to write poetry – a career choice guaranteed to drive even the mildest Cork parent to violence.

At that time Cork City Library had about two shelves of books on poetry and poets – mainly dead practitioners – tucked away in a seldom-visited corner of its imposing building on the Grand Parade. The meagre stock barely whetted my growing appetite. The only living poetry available was a series, about a dozen or so, of PEN Poetry Anthologies which I read from cover to cover and then began all over again, amazed and excited by the musical and visual range of poetic expression. Every weekend I searched through the even sparser poetry shelf in the Lee Book Store for something new. At school I'd found Keats and Blake. Now I was discovering Eliot, Pound and the imagists; Baudelaire and the French symbolists; Lorca and Neruda; Mayakovsky, Yevtushenko, Akhmatova; and a flowing electrical field of imagination and inspiration from the USA – Sherwood Anderson, Walt Whitman, The Spoon River Anthology, e.e. cummings, Dorothy Parker, William Carlos Williams, Kenneth Patchen, Jack Spicer, John Berryman, John Ashberry, Frank O'Hara, Hart Crane. These were the writers I leaned upon while dreaming of my own emancipation.

I stayed with the *Cork Examiner* for the next couple of years but my heart wasn't in it. That 'restless factor' gnawed away inside me like a living thing – some mysterious, unnameable motivator/enforcer that wouldn't go away – with a hunger that demanded more than poetry books or a couple of films every week. Many a sleepless night the feeling unnerved me. It would have been so much simpler to decide nothing, to sit at home at the end of every day and wallow in *The Songs of Leonard Cohen*. But trepidation about leaping headfirst into an unstable future paled beside the magnetic lure of poetry, and eventually – after much agonising and argument – I quit the *Examiner* and caught the boat, the *M.V. Innisfallen*, to London via Fishguard. Ironically, the decks were packed with young men who were sailing away in search of the kind of economic stability that I was leaving behind.

London's anonymity and its lack of moral constrictions suited me. To begin with I didn't write at all, simply allowed myself to be towed along from scene to scene, loving the aimlessness and living hand-to-mouth, as far from commitment and seriousness as was humanly possible. Poetry notebooks started appearing from 1973 onwards, filled with lyrics, spacey musings, teen-feverish love poems, and by 1975 I was writing in earnest, meeting and sharing/arguing ideas with other poets, bombarding poetry journals, small press magazines and newspapers with contributions, going through the whole acceptance/rejection process in an effort to establish a voice. Acceptances came trickling through from English-based publications such as *Aquarius*, *The Poetry Review*, *Bananas*, *Omens*, and the excellent *crackedlookingglass* broadsheet edited by Matthew Sweeney and Joe Malin, and from Irish-based publications like David Marcus's 'New Irish Writing', *Cyphers*, *The Stony Thursday Book* and *Poetry Ireland*.

Then, in 1983, Dermot Bolger, founder of the young-blooded and enterprising Raven Arts Press, accepted a bunch of my poems for *Raven Introductions 1*, and agreed, on the strength of the poems therein, to take a serious look at a first collection manuscript. Two years later, *The Restless Factor* appeared. It was positively received as 'an auspicious debut by a new young Irish poet', but in fact I was by then, as Anthony Cronin put it, 'a grizzled 33-year-old'. With its downbeat assortment of antagonists and protagonists, *The Restless Factor* was shot through with odd angles, suburban unease (in later collections this unease would develop into full-blown urban paranoia), figures of isolation, spectres of doubt and nervous uncertainty. It echoed my fascination with American dime-store mysteries and B-movies of the 1940s and set a stark lyrical tone that mirrored a mean-street perspective. By then I had learned that what is omitted from a poem is as vital as what is included.

Co-published by Raven (in Dublin) and Alison and Busby (in London), *The Way the Money Goes* (1987) received a Poetry Book Society recommendation. The collection emerged from an appalling mess; many of the poems had their genesis on scraps of paper, beer mats, empty Marlboro boxes, but were licked into taut shape with the generous and patient assistance of Bill Swainson, Alison and Busby's poetry editor. These poems had been fermenting for a long time – from the last years of the 1970s right up to the publication of *The Restless Factor*. As well as a time of personal upheaval, this was a time of huge social change in London. The refreshing, sneering innocence and anarchy of Punk rose and fell. Conservatism and cash now held sway in Thatcher's questionable democracy. The squatting scene, on which I had heavily relied for shelter, came crashing down. Rich incentives for the rich produced a feeding frenzy in which the poor were consumed. Council property was sold under the duped eyes of its tenants. Trade unions were undermined and destroyed. Wrecking balls were ever-present, everywhere. It was a grim, joyless time.

The Way the Money Goes was divided into two parts. The first part dealt with the break-up of a marriage; the second section focused on aspects of the city – cold basements, street hustlers, drug scenes, predatory developers, alienation and loss – as filtered through a vision in which all notions of love and redemption have collapsed. It was the last book to be published by Alison and Busby. They went bankrupt on the week in which I was to begin a series of readings that tied in with the UK publication. The London launch, to a packed house in The Poetry Society in Earls Court, was memorable and sad; part feast, part funeral. Afterwards a correspondent with the *Financial Times*, thinking maybe he had sniffed out an interesting story-link between the book's title and the publisher's misfortune, asked me, in all sincerity, if I had inside

4

knowledge of the company's situation. Man, I thought, I don't even have knowledge, inside or outside, of my own situation.

At the close of 1987 I fled from London to Dublin on a one-way ticket, in crisis. In Chinese there is a character which approximates the English word 'crisis', but instead of specifically denoting panic it can be understood as a turning point. Badly in need of repair and creative direction, I held this crumb of hope close to my heart.

Small Sky, Big Change (1989) was something of a hybrid. Many of the poems attempted to kick logic in the head, scraping backwards to a pre-cognitive understanding of poetry as sound and vision, instinctive and irrational. These were loose, rough-edged pieces in which the line between the real and the surreal, and the line between poetry and prose, were intentionally fuzzy. The end result has, I think, a firmly entrenched one-of-a-kind squalor.

Stark Naked Blues was published eight years after *Small Sky, Big Change*, a long gap in which, for the most part, I was zealously in pursuit of oblivion. I prefer to recall this collection as 'The Parkgate Book of the Dead' because of the locale where the bulk of it was written – the environs to the north of the Liffey, a sprawl of bedsits and cramped flats where I lived throughout the 1990s. I embraced life in this nowhere land, a transient among transients, a daylight ghost among daylight ghosts, as no more or less than I deserved. Strangely enough, it was this perspective of 'quiet desperation' which enabled me to revisit painful subject matter in poems such as 'Visiting Rights' and 'Lost Children'.

Renting a room – day in and day out, as weeks hurtled into months and months into years – was akin to renting a life. Every blessed thing, down to the smallest item of cutlery, was transitory, on loan only. Every morning brought the knowledge that one day the house keys must be returned. The concept of a future became redundant.

Sleepless nights and lengthy days were tinged with anxiety and regret. It was so easy to get lost in a seemingly endless span of time in which the mind did nothing but obsess over personal quandaries – in a place of inertia and inaction.

Then there were the others to contend with: the faceless tenants who came and went, each with his or her peculiar madness. The landlords who did nothing but pick up their cash or cheques on the button before dashing away from the deplorable sight of their crummy rooms. Entire lives fell apart on stair landings. Post and possessions went missing. Couples coupled and squabbled in plain sight. And these were just some of the ordinary occurrences. Let's not speak too much here of the substance abuse, the violence against women and children, or the mental illnesses that continued unchecked. Suffice to say that there is no correlation between the world we like to think of as 'normal' and the world as lived behind the walls of rented rooms.

Many of the poems in *Stark Naked Blues* and in *Looking in at Eden* (2001) came from dark seed, but it would be ultimately misleading and oversimplified to posit too many links between the content and the location in which they were composed. OK, 15 years in a bedsit was a long stretch, but as far back as *The Restless Factor* I was a poet of interiors, whose plodding beat ran, and still runs, from mind to room to street and back again, powered by imagination. An imagination that was itself propelled, a long time ago, by the moody black and white cinematography of cinema and the melancholy strains of old romantic songs, into private places of dream and longing where it continually struggles to express those weird feeling that tear away the artifice with which we cloak ourselves.

Aidan Murphy
Inchicore, Dublin
2007

Early Poems

The Massacre of the Innocents

They came while we slept.

I woke
and heard the sailors wail
for house and haven
as the sea-mouth opened
and swallowed their ships.
They battered the city gates –
and the treading
of their armoured boots on dry soil
knifed our children's dreams,
petrified our women's breasts,

sent scorpion and serpent scuttling.

Climbing Mount Zion in a daze
I heard the plunging
of well-honed swords
and the brazen cackling
of their childless hags.

Grey Poem

My birth was brightest grey.

It was greyer than northern cities.

It was shagpile cosy, textured
with the grey of forest floors
on misty mornings in November.

It was grey like rain on Sundays
in fishing-village harbours,
warmer than a turned-up collar.

With his grey distinguished hands,
into the sweet delight of grey existence,
into the grey misfortunes of war,
good Doctor Grey delivered me –
a racket made of wind and Cow & Gate,
a hula-hula baby in a grey Hawaii
all gaily bundled in my grey perambulator.

In this Restaurant
Princes Street, Cork 1971

In this restaurant I am sitting
by a window overlooking a narrow street.
I am inside a poem.
A tear rolls up and down my spine.
Schoolgirls are giggling.
They are beautiful, dressed in red and green.
They are so beautiful I climb out of the poem.
They do not notice the red ant earth
I shake from my body.
They do not notice the suicide
I see mirrored in the stainless steel sugarbowl.
They do not notice the pain
I feel approaching from a distance.
They do not notice.
They are giggling, exchanging ancient legends of love.
Their bodies are as open as ripe pears, but I am not hungry.
They talk of boys, dresses and dances.
They do not notice that I am a dancer.
They do not notice that my blood dances.

One
London, 18/2/1978

My son is one today. He doesn't know.
He's curious about my pen
moored above the page like a zeppelin
dropping stupid propaganda. I am trying
to make a circle with a broken compass.

Yellow taxi parked outside the Auto Shop.
Cold dealers handling fish and fruit,
staring through glass at dripping lambchops,
buying a slice of the average day.
My son is one. He yawns. He bites
a plastic comb with four front teeth.

I've just read *The First Elegy*
For The Dead In Cyrenaica. I am dumb.
Army jeeps cruise down the peacetime streets.
It's the elderly I feel for: the old
women with treetrunk legs trying to cross
the car-owned streets. With eyes of spooked deer.

My son cries. Pulls at my shirt and trousers.
Cranky, half-asleep, he bumps
his forehead on a chairleg. It's him
and others who are one I feel for now.
With their tiny faces and their tiny hands.
With their loud sleepy howls.

Fear of Fatherhood

November '79: stripped trees wept slush,
the endless traffic flattened it.
All night long the tyres crunched,
but the noisiest room was best for heat;
the other was fridge-like, asphyxiating.
No job, no prospects, petrified
I chewed my nails down to the quick.

Christmas hit me with a cheerless hammer.
I counted every penny, sleepwalking
wall to wall, imagining the worst.
Goblin voices in my head
tempting me to the frozen river.
Ice queens from childhood storybooks
coming to cage me in glaciers,
to test my faith with implements of darkness.

Then in February it thawed.
The rain came pissing down
and baby slithered from the womb.
Beautiful in a basket of firelight,
her swaddled heart emanating irrational wealth.

Naked Mask

You've used your final mask,
now you kneel on the edge of your 9th life.
The profile that survives can't be dismantled.
Its sallow surface full of sleep
is yours until your time is zero
and the cannibal clay inherits.

Walk away from this mirrored misery.
Get back to the ball.
Get lost amongst the gay who came as
horses, clowns, kings, starlets,
crooks and mandarins.
They'll adore your costume,
praise your face for authenticity,
compliment your choice of tragic tone.
Some will even ask you
for the maker's number.

You'll ache to say: It's real, I'm real.
But such a cry would only mar
the evening's sense of ease.

New Poems

Ray's Radio

Ray's gone, I don't know where.
I miss his all-night radio upstairs.
Through troubled, anxious hours
I coasted with closed eyes
along Ray's frequency, calmed
by his placid choice of station.
Those whispered broadcasts,
those underwater symphonies in gauze,
tucked me in, like a child
assured of safety in the dark
by adult voices downstairs long ago.

César Vallejo's Ghost

'César Vallejo is dead, they
nailed him down,
everyone did, though he did nothing.'

No,
César Vallejo still walks.
He can't go yet.
There is just too much to be forgotten.
He strolls along the alphabet.
He crushes the frozen snow of vowels and consonants.
He breathes a fog of immense pronouns.
The clouds that bind his bare feet
are no match for
the nails, the glass, the spikes.
But he bleeds no more.
His soul no longer suffers being his body,
and his passing, like a mountain view,
exhilarates,
emancipates,
reshuffles the whole world.

The Stoned Journal

It unnerved me for months.
It drew me in.
It possessed me.
My complexion paled.
My appetite stank.
There were too many stories to tell.
Too many angles on the info.

Clouded in smoke I worked on.
Pausing to refill my drink
I opened the window and door.
The backdraft burned pages 2 to 9.
I never noticed the dry ribbon.
Indecipherable
page after page on the desk.
Masterful and inkless.

I know I finished it
yet I have no proof.
It grew legs of its own as I slept.
Walked into the night without looking back.
Without a word.

Writer's Block

The shelves in my head
are stacked with blank papers,
virginal notebooks,
sentences that snap
like crispbread under scrutiny.
Speechless at the window
I witness the final sealing
of ancient settlements,
the old blocks disappearing
floor by floor, new structures
rising from the levelled waste,
gigantic steel maws
crunching stone and glass.

Life is so much better now,
I'm told. With its wide range
of placebos and dumb vocabularies;
with its dead safely under wraps;
with its attainable goals and
cold cash fueling the lights
of a globe gone dim from overkill.
But I'm like a man with fine boots
and no feet. If I knew
where the bank of passion was
I would empty its vaults,
liberate its currency –
but I cannot find a single word
for this new place, beyond extinction.

The Apathetic Anarchist

halfway through the making of the bomb
he falls asleep atop the pile of blueprints

he doesn't know what's come over him

                              even the plan
for the pharmaceutical hijack
no longer excites him

there are strong words he wants to say
harsh sentences he wishes to pass

but his tongue
might as well be severed from the root

and my
      my
      my
is the best he can muster

Voyeur in Black and White

Through the plateglass window of the Café Jacques,
shaking shiny droplets from her beach umbrella,
I watched her shelter from the summer shower
under the neon awning of the Ciné Pico.
She was smiling, waiting for her lover.

As he came striding to enfold her, diaphanous,
a rainbow curved above the river.
He kissed her lips and her little damp earlobes,
and when he asked her if she missed him she replied
'I missed you no more than I would my eyes.'

Long after they had gone, I sat there dreaming
of Acapulco in the days before piranhas of the dollar,
a stretch of white sand where love patiently waited;
and I sang out in praise of the power of two
to the metronomic tapping of my single shoe.

The Lantern

The lantern is lit.
Our naked bodies smoulder
on the closed drapes,
as blurred and fluid
as the waters of the *Leidsegracht*.

No-one who knows us
knows this place;
untouched, unblemished by memory,
each block and timber
tells a textless history.

Tastes and scents surprise.
And when I look into your eyes
I see another, resurrected.

The world's weight falls from your shoulders.

You pick it up and flick it in the bin.

The System

They give the boy
a free ride
a free lunch
a free taste.
It's what they always do.
Our masters. Our mentors.
Then –
with the cruelty of tradition –
they snatch it away
when it's longest
tastiest
sweetest.
They say it turns
the boy into a man,
but all it makes is one more
inmate of appetite.

Refugee Praying

He prays to forget

The redhot spires that punctured the rooftops of home

The bombs that leaked poison and wasted his legacy

The animal screams

of children plummeting into mass graves

He prays

To change his iron into feathers

To lay down his nightmares lighter than down

To learn from scratch the patient art of the newborn

Desert Island Discs

I zap the volume level and I dance
my lunacy across the kitchen floor.

The dead-on lyrics and the blissful beat
blow dead-end thinking into outer space.

Then, the first chords of a slow song
halt my limbering, sit me breathless down.

I turn to concur about the melody
with you, but you're not there,

only my tired palms,
my darkening sands.

A Holy Sixpence

To reach the house you cross
the city-centre in the harsh midwinter;
your shadows gash the frosted street,
dummies blaze in storefront windows.

You are four years old: Almost running
to coincide with your mother's sharp heels.
Your pocketed hand fiddles with a parer,
the other seeks out her warm sleeve.

At the house you are ushered
into candle light, a reek of incense.
On a high double bed a young woman, gone ancient,
is dying: Above her a giant with cataracts
conducts a requiem of smoke and whimpering.
The dying woman turns her northpole eyes
and crooks at you a breadstick finger,
and by the bedside presses into your little hand
a sixpence you can hardly wait to spend.

Black Maria

Above the sink
she shapes her lips
to a song on the wireless;
then stares from the window
at a crow surveying the earth
like a neck-starved hangman.

Scything the grass her gaze
stops dead at the lip of a trench
at the end of the lawn.
An iron cemetery:
a cistern,
a tricycle,
her mother's ancient range,
all enclosed by time and thorn.

Turning back to her washing
she doesn't see him there,
the frightened child,
the small boy
crouched among the briars,
in his stockade of stings
with a stick for a gun,
hiding from the passing
of the black oblong van
that has no windows.

The Boy with Jamaica in His Veins
i.m. Mark McCormack

Though they wrapped him in Caribbean colours
and burned his pain-cursed body
I dreamed last night I walked with him again
from Hill 16 to Capel Street
on up to The Furry Glen.
Life did him no favours.
In fact it crapped on him.
Being poor is never a walk in the park
but to be poor,
unskilled
and terminally ill
is one bucket more
than a bucketload of shit.
But did he complain?
Of course he complained. His anger
ignited his determination to keep struggling
as if he knew in the end
that he was bound to lose
but by hook or by crook
he would never be last.
And that's what we loved about him:
the barefaced cheek,
the sly glance,
the crooked laugh,
the studied, winning innocence.
He had a fire that could only be admired,
a way of seeing that occluded shadows,
a secret arsenal in his cancerous sinew,
like a cold-climate boy with Jamaica in his veins.

A Blaze of Glory

When you vanished, true gods vanished with you.
The blaze of your going stunned my poor astonished eyes.
For years afterwards, reliving your leaving again and again,
I was spellbound by the memory of your departure,
first a bird in a shuttered room, and then suddenly
the bracelets of your wings clasped light and air.
These days, between pangs, I laugh with the rest,
but never, even on my best, most pickled nights,
never have I burst as clean and free as you;
when you became an island without footprints,
when you were ripened to delight.

Crash

A fierce crush of metal brings me to the window –
two shattered cars, a pond of broken glass,
plastic spattered dark with blood.
Above the luscious trees
the swept blue guarantees
another day of rare heat.
I take a beer and sandwich to the stoop,
wait among the gatherers in summer light
for the whooping ambulances.
Here are faces I've not seen in months.
The ashen faces of one-room tenants.
The screwed-down faces of child-mothers
and the too-old faces of their doll-like broods.
The drug-glinting glee-faces
of outpatients in threadbare gowns and slippers.
The ominous masks of the tragedy gourmets.
Over walls and hedges
strangers pass comment to strangers;
their words imbued with an importance
that elevates them, momentarily,
above drudgery and loneliness.
Talking for the sake of talking.
Dreading the silence when the sirens go.

Jesus and Iodine

My maternal grandmother
believed wholeheartedly
in the curative power of iodine.
Praising Jesus
and cradling the little glass bottle
like it was pure gold
she painted my body all over
and spoke the word iodine
with the same respect and
reverence that she reserved
for His holy name.
Jesus and Iodine
Jesus and Iodine
ran like a breathless refrain
through my formative years,
her good Christian juju
keeping me safe
from devils and germs –
twin aspects
of the same old evil
in her village mind.

The Cowboy Suit

The rifle-stock is chocolate-coloured plastic.
Trigger and muzzle are cheap metal,
ersatz silver that peels onto fingers
like flakes of tinsel, poison to the tongue.

The vest is leatherette. I wear it loose
with mother's polka-dotted scarf
askew around my throat
just like I saw it on The Duke.

The boots are plastic too, dolled-up
with green lariats that droop;
and the stetson, a grey low-brimmed felt,
has a hole in the front.

Sometimes I wag my finger through that hole
to remind myself
that every day above ground is a good day.

On L. Cohen's 70th Birthday

At 17, on my hi-fi in the kitchen,
like a nutbrown coffin on a trestle,
I played you so often I tarnished
the grooves of your songs. In through
the door of your golden voice,
I wandered those bare, melancholy rooms,
tracing angel-footmarks in the dust,
waiting for my longing to be named.

At 21, you wafted from the windows
of bed-sits in Saint Luke's, where maidens,
hiding from the tedium of families,
hunted with verve for their souls.
I was fighting in the war between
the man and woman, all tangled-up
in limbs and lips night after night,
I thought my heart would shatter.

In my 30s, broken beyond repair,
I saw you in The Albert Hall, so cool
and calming with your voice, like sand
spilling through a child's fingers.
You were taking Berlin and Manhattan
with the ease of a boy Alexander,
preparing the bountiful banquet
for the return of the beautiful loser.

At 46, on Crete, I heard you crooning
by the pool. In the scented, balmy night,
the copulating cicadas joined
your Hallelujiah chorus, as it followed me
down to the dark shoreline,
tender as the sleepy, settling sea.

How can a man not care for music?
asked the water, singing round my feet.

Now here I am at 52, without a ticket
to the tower of song. Just waving you on,
in this room where the flares of your anthems
still light up the cracks in my travelogue,
still take me travelling in mind
to dwell upon love and its mystery,
and its sweet surrender to
the undeniable power of song.

The Price of Heaven

These merry little pranksters,
these sweet deceivers
I pop and swallow with gusto,
ride me tall in the saddle,
glide me right off the western skyline.

But I'll be down soon. Yes I will.
Down like a wind-up angel toy
on its last-gasp revolutions,
its tin wings clattering in vain
against the cold impassive clay.

Visitation Tour

Convinced he was adequately prepared to expect
the unexpected, he went south to the homestead
on a visitation tour. But – call it self-delusion –
he wasn't prepared at all,
he wasn't ready for the devastation.
Had he slept right through a world war?

He scanned the tableaux in the display cabinet
for the Chinese Empress and her maids-in-waiting,
but they'd scarpered with the glass dalmatians.
He hunted in vain for the Cuban cigar-box
that once held the blackwhite elastic-bound
handiwork of long-gone chemists.

Desperately he searched for one familiar thing,
a modest clue that he once lived here,
though nothing remained of the place he remembered.
At the end of the tour he would have settled
for a fake ghost or two, a few plastic skeletons,
even a single jigsaw-shard of acetate
snagged in the lining of a dead man's slipper.

Guts

when she returned
she soured the room

with graffiti of drowning
hands and burning bones

i thought i'd lost her
to some off-the-atlas hole

then came a steady
rising in her chest

each heartbeat stronger
than the one before

new blood irradiating
her fingers and toes

each glow brighter
than the glow before

one foot delicately
following another

guts   pink-
shining on her cheeks

Game Boy

This is the game, boy.

On either side of the road ahead
a variety of obstacles will shoot out at random.
Don't let the scenery fool you.
Don't, not even for a moment,
let the sky pull you in.
You must be ready to be one
with stone, with flesh, with plastic.
You must be prepared for
impact, collision, annihalation.

This is the game, boy.
Off you go now.

Snapshot

Between the pages of an old notebook I found a snapshot
of my son hunched over the rocking horse's neck,
stroking its dirty mane, its worn brown pelt,
with his four-year-old fingers.

How he loved that cheap beast!
For a couple of quid we hauled it
from the musty shadows of a junk-shop,
its rockers slightly out of beam,
the loose screws front and back making it rock off-centre.

How he rocked that long cold winter out!
Rocked the squalid room on its cowboy foundations.
Rocked until his cheeks glowed red from the electric heater.
Until his eyes drooped
tired and dazed from love's capacity.

Samurai Hedge Cutter

I am a Samurai hedge cutter.
Three times a day religiously
I polish my blade to a cutting edge
sharp enough to slice through bone;
but no-one calls me on the phone.

If I keep up payments on my advert
in the window of the local store –
and in the *Golden Pages*
under A for Arboriculture –
I will be bankrupt soon, before

I've had a chance to prove
the mettle of my sword. Some days
I wander through the suburbs –
my idle weapon hanging from my belt –
glaring at men with strimmers and buzzsaws

whose racket insults my silent profession;
knowing I could, with a warrior yell
and a sweep of burnished steel,
turn lush hedgerows into leafless stakes
and unruly bushes into lifeless meal.

On the Demolition
of the Arcadia Ballroom, Cork

The ghosts of the waltzing revellers are no match
for the bankers' bullies and their agents, so
shaking the dust from their Sunday best
they stagger from the ruins and wander
in pairs towards Kent Station.
Some head south and some head north.
A couple float Chagall-like
over the abandoned mills.
The rest dance into the city centre
and foxtrot in the hollow shopping malls
or take their shoes off and recline
on the steps of the Capitol Cineplex –
all their spirits fading into summer's end.

Stuff

When it's time for a change, you forget
that things are sometimes better undisturbed.
Do one room, you're compelled to do another.
Decorating gathers momentum, like fast-forward tape.
The new floor mocks the wall.
The brackets misfit and mismatch.
The ceiling is drab like never before.

So, you rearrange and shift.
You pull out portions of the past.
But you can't stay uninvolved,
like some paid removal man,
and stuff, buried for years,
creeps up from behind
and roots you to the spot.

There's no end to it; no final sorting.
That chair, that rug,
that bracelet from the blue.
Old letters, keys and photographs;
the surprising paraphenalia of your life
will hound you out the door, all the way
to the other side of the world.

2 NCR D7

Goodbye NCR D7,
the concrete heart
that took me in
when bleeding hearts did not.
When I met you
death and devils were upon me,
sniggering and taking measurements
as I arced towards perpetual winter.
But you pillowed my fall;
you opened my eyes
and poured the cream in;
you freed my ears
of funereal noise and tuned me
back among the living.

Farewell long avenues of trees
that blossomed and shed
the years that sped too fast.
How will I ever sleep again
without the screech of burning rubber
or the armies of wasted voices
screaming, fighting, loving,
weeping, dawn to dawn?

So long, saloon-keepers
and professional drinkers.
Let me raise this half-full glass
to the many who stepped outside
for a minute and never returned –
to the handful who remained
steadfast in decay, twisting
in the wind of advancing cranes –
and to all the crestfallen who fired
my faith in the ordinary day.

The Dead Don't Like to Linger

The dead don't like to linger.
Like babies just learned to walk
they bee-line for the nearest door
through which they may wander.

But the living hold tight to the reins.
Fretful and anguished, the baffled
survivors keep poking remains and
running old footage over and over.

If someone could hear them
the dead would cry out:
'our dying is done
the hard work is over
we don't like to linger'.

Why then do you keep them
clenched in your fists
among the chains and padlocks
of each living day?

From

The Restless Factor (1985)

Whistling

The man going home alone
stares intentionally at nothing
and whistles. In bed I hear
his song of concentrated terror,
the tension of controlled breath.
It is a million years ago.
Axe in hand he wades in slime,
slugs bubble at his knees.
Somewhere in the wet forest
another advances, a perfect
double; his own armed and
cautious image, whistling
as he whistles, notes of fear.

Is this what music is, this
gentle Schumann spinning here,
snowing on the world? Is it
born of an old reluctance,
a turning from silence and self?
I feel relieved. The symphony
is over. And the man? The street
is empty, his tune gone.
Under the sheets I watch
lights fencing with the dark.
Pins are dropping on the quilt.
I purse my lips and blow.

Friendship

You know the painting I mean –

two naked men stretched between
heaven and earth's brilliant extremes,

veins and muscles straining
to link limbs. And it continues
beyond the frame. The bodies writhe,
struggling to cancel struggle,
to be whole and single.

But who gets to make the breakfast?
And who gets the much-needed rest?
And round two breaks
whose bloody heart?
                    Still
it is a free-for-all,
and when you see something you want
you climb up on his shoulders.

Or, one serene night in the shrubbery
he reveals himself, and you reassure
his hand before the door closes.

And tomorrow you break your heart
trying to remind him.

Appearances

Minus your blabbing and the radio
the wind comes through like a jet wheel.
Swooping from every window breach it focuses
my attention on holes I'd never seen –
cracks in the cupboard, cracks in the stair.
Is anything safe when the talking stops?

Tonight they are gone down the valley.
I cannot see them in this coat of fog.
I pace alone the rooms we pace by day, but now
suspicious of the rattling latch,
suspicious of the dark green trees
like nervous sentries watching from the plain,
I step from room to room without a gun,
wary of sound. And no-one speaks.

A Small Blind Street

anna sang light opera
her daddy played the piccolo
her mammy watered the raspberries

celia snuffed her nostrils black
sat half-dead in a parlour bed
her ears plugged to a noisy radio

jacko shinned up lightpoles
in pursuit of phantom kaisers
punched his eldest in the bolted toilet

and every morning hail or shine
pa the spa dragged
his game leg to mass
and on summer evenings shovelled
hot horseshit

the intricate existence
of that small blind street
went in my eyes and out
like a threaded needle

i am still embroidered with
its lunacies and contradictions

After Hours

The lights of the boudoir, dead.
Scent of bottled lilac, fag-ash.

The spirit-level shakes her still
as she removes her clothes.

The customers have left the street
to Winter. Hungry seed-eater.

The pistol has been tucked in
its drawer. Vice is
less than a nameless sound.

Tomorrow the papers will have it.
On trains the legible offal
will change between stations,
truth crushed in the engines.

She is not interested in tomorrows.
Standing naked by the window.

Torture

You want him to go, you want to
exhume the dead areas. When you bathe
you avoid the full-length mirror,
not wishing to see the child-bearer.

You stand at the gate in the sun
becoming the flat horizon;
you lie under the cherry tree
until you're small and red,
ready to fall. Even the radio is
a door you exit,
escorted by popular music.

He returns like a stubborn shadow.
Hoping to change his mind
you increase your demands,
subtly stripping him
instead of spitting in his eye.
You don't want him here
but won't say Go: he must cast
the first stone.

But he binds tighter,
sings as he waters the roots.
Soon you will learn to enjoy
the brief absences of pain
he cleverly grants you,
like all great torturers.

His Gift

The pillow under her head
is charged with her dreaming,

but the voltage is quite mild tonight,
and when she sends out her messages
the vibration of the feathers
is almost imperceptible.

Gently into his hands
he controls their passage,

to save them for the day
she needs them
to survive.

Tourists

Our brochures and maps are useless.
They describe another country,
somewhere averse to change, not this
transient state of shifting earth
we dare not stir, burdened with
wads of play-money and tin keys.

We try to beat the mood,
rise early, make lists of possible moves.
But the wind here is a hunter of plans,
blowing the soil with the shreds
of our thoughtful strategies.

We stop struggling. The native gods
are too powerful. Absurd to go on
with this contest between terrier and bear.
We sprout fungus under the clock,
waiting for time to terminate
our rash contract, waiting for reprieve.

Meanwhile we sit at this window,
mostly silent. It's a restless view
which affects us – we're less flesh,
more water. Perhaps we're about to be born,
perhaps we'll rise into the air and laugh
at the mess we made being here.

Kid Blood

Early in the day
when birds are dreaming
see how fast he wakes,
how eagerly he takes the teat,
like an everlasting magnet
pulling new attractions,
more of anything existing,
more, clockwork encore,
planets in his hand,
moon garnished with constellations.

Look at him, Old Man!
His crowing wakes the cock
and startles sun-up. Look at him!
Your heir is innocent of heavy tongues,
his breast immune to envy, vengeance.
The undefiled potential in his clawing fist,
his bright inquisitive eyes outshine
your treasuries. Look at him, Old Beaten Dog!

Does he nullify the profit of your cunning deals?
Do you rage like Herod fearing loss of pence,
demand the infant spiked, spitroasted?
Or do you, stooping, lay your arms
at his feet and slip backstage
less certain, less encumbered.
The choice is yours:
his flesh to love or burn.

Either way, Old Veteran,
your days are threshed. This is,
think carefully, your last decision.

Touching Parallels

All night I dug for a reasonable word,
a perfect verse handknit from salvage,
a poem you might wear on a cold night.
Now my notebook bulges with atrocity,
the diary of a sick, unfeeling species.

I want him on the line.
My guilt wants to parley with his.
My mouth wants to sing in his ear.
I dial. The phone rings ...

Who'll deny this is a wicked moment
but there is no other; this fact assists
my breathing down the deaf shell. (He's
in the shower, a wet towel trails
across the tiles. Caked with soap
his hand is closing in on the receiver.

and it freezes there. The instrument,
silent in its cradle.) Clients queue
outside, waving coins, itching
to pile into these upright tombs
for shots of hope. It's a poor service,
most will fail,

        strangled by ruthless tapes;
        shamed by cybernetic language;
        doublecrossed by gadgetry that
        never weakens or desires.

Hart Crane

Underneath a sycamore
a fat lady waits
for you to come to her
with bags of promised oranges

But on the ocean bed
below this land of sense
absent from light and shade
neither wet nor dry
unaffected by squall or calm

You are suspended motionless
preserved in salty void
with no memory of the colour
or the shape or taste of fruit

While gulls bear wriggling fishes home
and ships bear anxious boys
towards adventure and old age

The fingers of the wind unlace
and lace the ancient lady's bonnet

Procession

Here comes the screeching owl
9 days without a shave,
grim and old and broken,
homesick for a past of figures,
voices he can't summon anymore.

Here comes the shadow-caster,
self-fabricator. The beast
the whore finds irresistible,
the doom behind desire. And
here's the information-sucker,
shabby stranger, patron
saint of nausea, Odysseus
on a bad trip (this time
ravished by the lotus eaters).

Here comes the inquisitive skull,
the clitoris feeding on geometry,
this year's Miss Lust,
last year's Miss Lunacy. Hot
bitch with deuces up the sleeve,
who bathes in concept, who
rabid spews the picked
bones of achievement.

Here's the walking billboard
advertising Kali Yuga (no tuppence
ha'penny Fred or Harry's Diner).
They have lived underground like outlaws,
but now's the hour to scavenge
the final plain. Here they come –

here's Cancer, here's the Laundress
Of The Labyrinth, in whose automatic
miracle the washday world spins. And
Look! Blind Newton leading Crazy Jane.
Now we're all here,
trying to widen a stiff lens.

Snow White

On the white enamel sink
my goodtime powders dry,
my crimson stick retreats
into its golden shell.
Longlegged spiders drag away
my false eyelashes.

In the dirty mirror
blonde and dim, my face,
split like a dried-up
waterhole, gropes
for a sign of beauty,
settles for a tint of recognition.

I ache behind the eyes, the ears
hallucinate a nail thud-
thudding into leather, my
hard skin feels its
cruel point, the warm
trickle of blood.

I walk from hall to kitchen;
it's not like moving. Maybe
I'm dead – at best a
smokepuff curling from
some stranger's skull,

most real when I fall asleep
and dream of happy marriages,
or those long-forgotten ski-
trips on the mountains of America.

Lightning

Not sleeping
not awake
between the ceiling
and the floor some
faculty composed a poem
I should remember.
A cold key on
the tip of my tongue
teasing my thirsty heart.
Like the flesh
of an old flame sealed
in a crypt of smoke
the form hides in everything
I touch and like a flash of
lightning vanishes on contact.

I wish I had more meat
and less obsession   my visitor
is either out there dreaming
or in here scouting and
he wants what I want
definition and resolve to be
so tightly welded
no-one notices the scar.
We are strangers
waiting to appear.
We might be mortal enemies.

1%

'What earthly use,'
you ask, 'this tiny figure,'
but I won't let go my
1% for none but one.
Jeer, call me crazy,
phone the institute to
crack me under pressure,
1% stays mine –
that constant lowly
sum I earned honestly.

You take greedily
your 99%, plunge pirate
hands up to the arms
in wells of earth, squabble
over corpses' teeth,
pluck the planet's green
fur, tuft by tuft, baring its
thin neck to a foxy moon.

Strike me from your
escalating graph – can't
use my 1% for gain. It's
not cold as coin
nor rough like ore – it's poor,
shifting windblown sand
around my heart.
It's formless,
ragged to your spruced eye,
timid beside your snarling cavalcades,
unimpressive, but you'll never kill it.

1% endures
to pay the ferryman
to carry me (one day
with love) across a choppy sea.

The Country of the Blind

At Blindman's Bridge, bereft of possessions,
they're herded into seat-stripped tubes.
Crushed, they sway through miles of tunnel,
faces at the windows like fish in striplit tanks.
Once they reigned in sunlight,
sired wizards and inventors.
Once they were fastidious gentlemen with futures;
enemies fled when they sang. Now, they're singing
to keep dark possibilities at bay,
but their voices are timid, wounded,
and many have no tongues at all.
No track runs back; no water-hole ahead;
no honeycomb of facts in which to swarm;
no gods to guard them from deceiving moons.
The melody is cracked.
The past is pawned, without redemption.
Destination-labels pinned on their wrists –
square white cards, blank on both sides.

The Virus

Whose sons are these
whose features are not ours?
Some alien cuckoo screwed our wives
but when? And why?

We try to smother them at night,
we try to drown them at bathtime –
what force prevents us?

All our gods are dumb.
In vain our supplications scrape
their painted surfaces.

Reply to the Ostrich Foundation

I'm happy here in the leper colony,
with boiled clocks, clouds and agony.

I've burned the bridges you sent me,
the flame was precious while it lasted.

Now, I'm educating my head
to stay out of sand,

and I sleep quite soundly
with the blacker sheep. Herewith

I'm obliged to refund your sanity.
Having checked the contents

I am not impressed. So, stuff
your olives and your Parker Pens.

I'll not tolerate inclusion
in your wingless catalogue.

The Mark

You are not immune;
there is no safety in Paraguay
or alpine chalets. Streets,
rooms, caves; you might as well
be naked on a high roof
pounding your chest like Kong.

Do not think yourself inconsequential.
Do not think yourself innocent.
A fast car is coming and
your scent hangs upon the wheels.
You have done nothing
to deserve this, nothing; but
this too is a punishable offence.

The Restless Factor

Whoever he was
he checked out in a hurry.
Why did he leave like that
having booked so far in advance?
Something in the room
is left unsolved. Something
not quite as crude
as a corpse in the wall,
but near enough.
The book-spines are still warm,
the smoke I blow seems
scripture in the atmosphere.
I'll be here until I've proved
there is no evidence.
A lifetime job.

From

The Way the Money Goes
(1987)

The Way the Money Goes

Because of her sparkling eyes
he guessed a sour ending
but he went along with her
for the sake of the game
and because just like now
he had nothing then except
a mental map of the big smoke
and some lousy photographs.

And now although he wishes
for the patience and the power
to describe what happened
between there and here
he settles for shorthand.

Sex. Poverty.
The way the money goes.

Written in Water

The taste of the rational man
in his element is clear,
daring in colour and form.

He discriminates and selects
with an eye for the solid goods.

Therefore I must be deranged –
afraid to touch you
lest you not be there.

The Meeting

They met between memories, each
surprised by the presence of the other,
wary, tense, unsure of a frail element.
But neither wanted battle here, only
peace to forget the betrayed children.

She cried for his shattered power, for
the ancient hunter lost to commerce.
And he cried for the coarseness of her hands,
and the light that was ebbing.

Noon

This is always the worst hour.
She breaks awake so fast
the room clings to her gown.
Sipping coffee bitter and black
she watches through silk haze
the crows on the shorn lawn,
the convoys twisting uphill
like mutant mambas, remembering
the strong arm that held her.
But the arm comes with the shoulder,
the neck, and the face she despises.

Penultimate Ceremonies

I smash the albums,
kick the cat,
graze my knuckles
on the kitchen sink.
My hairy arms bristle.
It is time for the harness.

I'm sick of remembrances,
tired of kissing
life into a drowned mouth.
This place, this here-and-now
is curdling my skin,
turning my tears into lard.

I want to eat her alive,
I want to curse her womb,
I want her to suffer
the fate of a lobster.
Instead I inch across the carpet
on the crutches of my fists,
towards the light.

Sense of Loss

In dreams now
she is always missing.
Have you seen her?
I ask wall-builders,
fence-menders, roof-tilers.
They know more
than they admit.

My mother comes to me
with her feet on fire.
The one you needed most,
she says, you swapped
for a broken bugle.

Life's structure changes.
    Vapour,
    glass,
    cold twilights,
without my gentle sherpa.

Come Back, Miss Natural!

Come back, Miss Natural!
My days are too civilised.

I long for your temper.
I dream of your scowl.

These pot-plants,
this delicate China,
this elegance is tedious.

I want to sleep again
between your claws.

My mind's in splints, hobbling
from clock to telephone,
stoned on soap and fluids.

Come back!
Soil the carpet!
Make it fly again!

Declaration of Independence

My house is devastated
my children are peculiar
my wife is vicious

I need chemicals
my vocabulary is minimal
my time is arseways

My face is puffed with fat
my cock is on the dole
my motor is worthless

My theme is incoherent
my ass is beautiful
my hands are spotless

My phonecalls are tactless
my poverty is painful
my critics are numerous

My file is thick
my tobacco is strong
my bodywork is scratched

I kiss like a woman
my instinct is muscular
my gifts are hidden

My mother is a nuisance
my home is mythical
my reading is limited

My mistress is dubious
my plans are tattered
I have a nightclub passion.

Bonsai

While you were mixing drinks
in the kitchen, I don't know why
I opened the top drawer
of your bedroom-dresser.
Inside a forest sprouted,
treetops almost level with the rim.
Before you returned I closed it
and never said a word. Nowadays
knowing I could have loved you better
it stars in my imaginings –

I see your forest on a scales,
I see you plucking its leaves
with a black tweezers. One night
I dreamed I had a dresser of my own.
Inside I'd built a tall city
of steel and glass, where
people levitated over snow,
hunting needles. I weighed
my city against your forest,
watched them seesaw slower, slower,
till both came to rest
on an even keel of sky.

Minus Three Degrees

Among the fashions of the dead sister
I dream of artichokes,
my wife on stumps.

'The coldest February for 40 years' –
Lammy sleeps in a dirty overcoat.
Above us, the speed-freak
topples the dresser,
screams himself hoarse
as he smashes the TV.
His mother is obese. Her feet
pinched into high boots
clatter across the floor.
One day she slipped on the snow
and couldn't rise; she spat
on the black man's offered hand.
Huddled around the one-bar flame
the old lady whispers –
'the developers are coming'.

Basement

One of us procrastinates,
one is slowly dying,
one is sick with loneliness.

We have grown accustomed to whispering,
to skirting each others' eyes.
We peep through lace curtains
at the interminable rain
rolling to the drain, watch
the sparrows skip the crusts
that we have spiked with codeine,
the ants perishing on salted steps.

In the shed there is a beehive
made from bits of cushion-foam.
Yesterday we sprayed it with Ralgex,
laughed as the workers shrivelled.

Today the Bengal market burned to the ground.
Outside, bedraggled in the lightning,
the preacher swore it was the torch of Christ.
Tonight the Roscommon man brought beer
and spoke of trees and leaves,
gesticulating with his calloused hands
like the Hollywood cowboy he could have been.

Niagara Falls

Somewhere to be, not alone ...
We arrive from Sioux Bend –
you in your mother's costume,
the slimming grey number
with the beaver-trim collar,
me in showboat stripes,
slouch hat and leather tie.
We embrace on the porch
as the Falls crash down,
the surging slowing our moves –
so I imagine, briefly,
a quietness in our desire.

How many days went by? Remember
going home in a trainload of honeymooners
to Sioux Bend, Salt Flats, Red Rock,
Elksville; then, the children born
followed the railroads,
blew away with the smoke of big cities,
hearing perhaps their own unlikely Falls
in Fords and Ragtime. We died, of course –
someone discovered Angel Dust ...

and still the water goes over the edge,
and change or no change
an ear is waiting to hear,
a mind is eager to reveal,
what makes this battered flesh so special.

The Spoils

Over here
out of sight of the door
the punters are spilling
the stolen goods.

Shirts in cellophane and duvets
mingle with video software
and Big Dora's tally of steak
and Russian caviar.

Out of the smoky back-booths
comes the noise of trading
and short tempers; the violent
pride of thieves;

I can hear, but not see,
knuckles smashing through bone,
a pool-cue splintering on flesh,
and a woman screaming for a ceasefire
that will never be realised.

Cinema

Men with gaping mouths
and dazzled women shuffle
in the queue outside
the pocket atlas store

A black car
circles the block
the driver counts the laps
with horn-blasts
97 ...98 ...99

Beside each other
in the cinema
they cast their hooks
at the screen
their lines do not tangle

That inch between their elbows
is the Grand Canyon

Flypaper Terrace

The world, mythical and real,
was just beginning to appeal.
She counted cities on her fingers
like the young Alexander.
Night and day belonged to her,
no-one and nothing contained her.
She roamed the town and country
like a queen – unafraid,
curious, learning strange customs.
She rented a room in the city
near the river on a steep hill.
She covered the mouldy walls
with black and white reproductions –
Beaton, Brandt and Warhol – killing
the must with the scent of herself,
changing the sexist landlord
into gibbering plasma.
She owned a Leica and a hundred dreams.
She lived on Quaker Oats, chewing
to the soundtrack of Emmanuelle.
She fed the swans across the bridge,
explored the sidestreets, drawn
by a primitive music. And she found
the hangout of the lost,
the kingdom of chewed nails, and
fell in love with the arch-loser.
He crushed her future in a wild embrace,
gave her a little bastard
and a uniform of sawdust.

A Death in the Family

I speak of the weather
the blue forecasts
Sunday's comical newsreel.

She lies still.

I speak of the old street
when life was less desperate
of the plough in the sky
like a new saucepan
and the fragrance of fuschia.

Briefly she smiles. Then
remembering all the buried boys
her face shuts like a fist.

I sit there, a voyeur,
willing my hands to behave.

Doctor and priest come in,
a pair of village idiots.

Mammoth

I'm not the vogue –
hair is out,
largesse is out.
When penetrating jungles now
it's fashionable to be silent.

Without class,
without style,
what can I do? I stomp around,
I fuck up deals
simply by being there.
I sweat persistently
despite the cool foliage.
Can't even get it on
with my own kind,
who have taken, like me,
to the caves on the high slopes.

I press my bulk against a rock.
My legs fold like a deckchair.
My eyelids drop like anvils from a height.
Vaguely I hear motions in the world –
not my business, I don't care
who's whooping it up out there,
who's lording it over the lesser mammals.

I'm not up to it anymore,
the offspring pain me,
my skill is gone.
My eyes and ears are closing,
falling into a lurid sleep.
Hope nobody finds me. Ever.

I'm Glad that You're Rejoicing

I'm glad that you're rejoicing,
yours must be a pleasant house.

I imagine two towers – one
for sunrise, one for sunset,

and a stream of large windows
for the idle hours in between.

A fortunate man indeed! Living
in such a radiant climate,

with so many household thrills
to eulogise; a charming wife,

and a child in a spotless frock
poised like a model in a meadow.

Everything's fine here too –
the rain's washing mud from the pane

and the head-wound is healing well,
and as you say, who am I to complain?

Life on Funny Farm

No eggs, no bananas,
and positively no alcohol.
I am a window-man, one
who watches with envy
the marked cattle.
I must also be quiet,
especially at visiting-time –
must sit with folded arms,
an exhibit, a Zen adept.
I keep secret diaries:
Tales from the days
of virgin blood and daisies
when I had wind in my thighs
and a mouth like a bullwhip.
None of the pack would
recognise me now – my belly
wobbles when I walk the yard,
my head's a pumpkin
dark behind the eyeholes.
They are pleased with me.
I have come far, progressed
from wolf to whippet, can now
I'm told, be easily managed,
will soon be allowed
on the holy bus (shoes off
at the door, no smoking).
What kind of life is this
for a natural gangster, or
for any man who claims
to be his own master?

From

Small Sky, Big Change (1989)

Slices of Savoury Lion

1.

'I'm leaving
and I won't be back,'
she said, and stood there
wanting her knees hugged,
her back slapped, wanting me
dragged through the dust
to the end of the stairs.

Once she might have been that lucky,
I, that desperate.

'I'm leaving
and I won't be back.'
'Aren't we all,' I said,
turning back to the tasty mane of myself.

2.

Courage, sister; courage:
a little unease is essential.
Let's bury the hatchet, burn the spear,
go blind back into the beginning
where the country is not soft or fierce
but defiant of description.

I'm gagging on opinion. I'm sick
of the mouths going dark/light, dark/light;
the everyday reports and rumours;
blank eyes at the door at all hours
and sour breasts.

My tail is lit.
Your hands on my wrist
tell me it's the right time.

3.

I hear I'm still being talked about –
as one brings up the subject of a lousy movie
and the entire room goes daft on its defects.
It is noon. I am climbing
the tree again
with my paw in my mouth,
removing the bones
of your kind of people.
Affected by instants now,
by wild birdcalls,
by the tones of the wind and the way
the forest swells and festers,
who needs the goodwill of the righteous?

I have earned my pelt,
suffered for my roar.
Alone I know I am
the animal of my dreams.

The New Arrival

That final day was warm and bright
but he was dark and frozen
in a trenchcoat, damp and caked in clay.
The scissors in his fist was red
blood ran from the remnants of his hair
and his right hand stank of the baby's ass.

He had morphine in the brainpan,
brandy in his bark, when he heard
the voices crying fool, fool, fool –
but he was too far out
on a pygmy raft of his own design,
too far out to be no dream.

Money he said – Gimme money,
and someone crossed his palm
with paper, a oneway ticket
via first class shock, not negotiable.

First thing he did when he arrived
was buy a map of the new city
which he studied with his good eye.
Soon, he thought. Soon I'll walk.

Small Sky, Big Change

One red shoe,
a bloody shirt,
and the wedding's over.
I join the hangdog heads
where promises fly
and stick to beer-stained wood.
The saga continues. She
of the dark hair
cut with a hatchet
wobbles in the doorway.
It is not quite day
nor is it night – the light
at the window
is more a point of view
or like the wiseguy said
the soul's forever darkest
at four in the morning.
Relax I tell her
they're closing the shutters –
but she chokes and moans
about the men who've
bolted from her life
leaving only burned houses,
how she misses her nightbirds
her ducks and her mad dogs.
Life – she scoffs – it's nothing
but small change under a big sky.
And dare I say vice versa?
The deer's head on the wall
looks down at me
with its blank beads.

The Catalyst

You are nits in a wig
singing praises of hair.

You see façades, bland packages,
never the miracle powder in the day's false bottom.

The catalyst waits.
The catalyst is always here,

patient in spite of the pus that squirts when you speak,
hoping and praying that the child-eating hag

will be tamed by a spell in the oven,
that light will fall finally equal on all.

Scorpio Rising

Slowly she peels
the black lacy glove
and hits a vein.
Beside her
stinking of booze, with my mind
on the poison of marriage,
I watch her glow.

Leaning her spiked hair
against my chest, she says,
be my cautious old man, talk magic,
and stroking her lobes I fill
the squalor with my voice,
its blah blah blah a bier that lowers her
into the sleep that's like no other.

I study the urchin figure in my arms,
her classical pallor, thinking
how easy it would be now
to squeeze the life from her throat –
much easier than waiting
and mourning
her slow, shameful waste –

but I stay as I am; then
remembering my own abusive history,
our scorpion affinities, I hold her
closer, tighter – her poor, dumb daddy.

The South American Powder Room

It's cosy at Christmas
in The South American Powder Room,
with the steep red bank of the fire,
the parasol twirling on the ceiling,
and the rich green portraits.
Outside, the lawn is gouged
by rain that folds
brown sheets upon the river,
but here it's all tinsel and snow,
each to his own dilation,
each to his own flaming soul.
The abandoned waterfront
is a graveyard of unopened crates,
two ships in darkness
wait like beggars for a handout,
one window burns in the flour mill;
but death and decay
are not in question here,
we're stone monkeys who don't care,
we're the ancients snorting the present,
skimming over the scum; in here
tomorrow's not another day.
It's cosy at Christmas
in The South American Powder Room.

Cathedral

'Were there a God
and in the flesh
and could he call me, I would
walk around, I would
wait a little.' – Johannes Bobrowski

Your house is mighty Lord,
I'm plankton in its gloom.
Effulgent windows shed on me
a mood of doom no flame
or flower could alleviate,
like a tank full of dead bugs
exuding gases I can't breathe.
So Lord, excuse
my reluctance to kneel,
it's oxygen I need, not awesomeness;
and on this pigstuck planet, please
allow me this unworthiness:
I too prefer to walk around
and wait a little.

Exorcism

He is gone from my dreams.
With his grey listless fur.
With his spittle and his pocked skin.
With his terrible din of unhappiness.

He is gone from my shabby wardrobe
to spit his sugar mice elsewhere,
to trade his guesswork for another's disbelief,
to scratch some coast, thank Christ,
a million miles from here.

He is gone, my rotten accomplice,
back to the lightweight archway,
back to his beads and his safety helmet,
back to unwind love's stinking bandage.

And I at last am where I belong,
frying neglected fish in this imperfect climate.

Love Curse

May you cry twelve dozen tears
In the solitary confines of a square
Tantalised by beauty leering cruelly
Out of reach in one corner

And may your tears turn to flames
That blister your eyes
And force you to see
Twelve dozen variations of yourself.

The Lonesome Index

when i lift the latch
that old man
father of my mother
is back on the corner stool
with a bum's long hair
and a sharp eye
bluer than an optrex cup
spieling a new complaint
asking forgiveness in his foxy way
some drink and food
the bed beneath saint teresa
and in those cajoling eyes
especially those wet spongy lips
i see the mother of my mother
washing and singing
and opening bags of english gifts
and suddenly the house
is one triumphant roar
the most wonderful surprise party ever
even my old pal who lost
the best part of his skull
says the joke's on you murph
life goes on and on
nobody ever dies
we're always here
always handy on the lonesome index

Lessons in Pouting

Look
she says
passing me the magazine

It's a series
of lip photos
seven lessons in pouting

In next week's issue
there's a free tear

Better buy it
I say
in case we're moved.

The Girls

The girls
are dialing for Jesus.
The pleasures
of the flesh
are not enough, they sing,
the bones get tired
and the need
shuts its trap.
Now they're tapping
on the wires for Christ,
for someone
with a solid proposition.
I'm just the Friday cleaning-man.
When I meet them in the hall
I step over their bowed heads,
avoid their eyes.

Amateur Voodoo

The sky at night is wired,
mined with gods.
In the silence you can hear
the dogmas bicker,
the gumsy against the bearded,
the masked shouting down the feathered.
They want you; they want you
bright as a circus seal. They want your mouth
to open wide for their dim slivers,
unable to speak,
unable to refuse to praise
and kiss the rooster's headless stump.

I know you're scared. You're frail and lost
among these sharks and laserbeams,
with the whole world flailing, and worse,
those creatures that squat in the memory.
I know how huddled and confused you are
by products screaming, buy me, try me, bite me.
But the telephone keeps ringing in the Porsche
and no-one comes to wipe the sweat away,
though you have weighed them with bundles
and plagued them with fresh blood and candles.

The Lady in the Bag

This is her time and this is mine
and like it or not
I do what I can
to her skin with my hands
to kill the trembling
as she in her goodness
spills milk on my trifling concerns.
But old movie tickets
and capless lipgloss and foreign coins
spill out when she's angry
and a cloudlike gum clings to her hair
and melts over the pale peaks of her face
and I wish I could reach through the dark pockets
but I know too well where we stand
each on a meagre lozenge drifting away.

From

Stark Naked Blues (1997)

Sanctuary

When I walk in the door
they smell my dismay.
It's cool, son, they say,
we have been here forever.
And it's true. Whatever your crime
there is someone here who did it.

These are living mirrors,
these are my dour accomplices,
these are my brothers who laugh
for the sake of the sound of it.
Step inside, Greta,
don't be bashful,
there are diversions here
amongst the wreckage.

Soon, the joint fills,
and as the woods of pain encroach
we keep our needles clean, pointed,
ever-ready with jolts of light
and slick, surreal yarns. In here
the main event is over,
the palaver is done: So

don't cry, hon, the torches of dawn
were never as bright
as the sun in your heart,
and the names we might have made
less solid than this swirling ice.
Known by all and none
let this be our raft of the moment,
bobbing on these queasy waters
not-so-young lovers anymore.

Night Painting

Low in the river
the swans are sleeping
with their necks tucked
under oil-spattered wings

A drunken car swings
uphill through the fog
and out the rolled-down glass
a waitress pukes

In doorways the young
are kissing   holding hands
bathing in imaginary seams
and unzipped jeans

Mascara'd witch
the city blinks
bubbling and brewing
stews of trouble

In the back of the Volks
I touch your bruised thigh
as you raise the open bottle
to my parted lips.

The Year of the Wind

In the year of the wind
I was miles from the heartland,
goon-eyed under a crooked vine
with nothing to write home about.

The world was out of season –
a long street of gales and swooping leaves
in an age of urchins bawling
over dirty redbrick balconies,
and blue lights cutting corners
arresting intrigue.

There was vagueness everywhere:
multi-channel days
and nights of stunned silence,
profundity doused in a lather
of crude jokes and neat scotch.

And death was a cheeky pup
pacing your roof,
stuffing its maw
with chunks of misfortune.
Getting heavier above your head.
Getting heavier above us all.

Telegram

worn to a thread from sacrifice
he went north
to the mountains to rest
and there
in one agonising motion
of planetary jive
he died

he never said
or did
anything of consequence
nothing
nothing but a light blowing out
as the wind rolled in from the bay
and the stars dripped down
extraordinary calm.

Waiting Room

The yellow-vested yankee
and his thousand-dollar wife
are reading *Life*. Junior
rabbit-bites a chocolate square.
Cigarette smoke screens the window
from trainless tracks, strips
of neon stitching stone and steel.
On the wall-bench
finished crosswords curl up
under the hot air fan,
among suitcases, cameras, plasic bags.
An old man shuffles in
carrying a wizened brown case
trebletied with scraps of string,
sits and pulls out black beads,
prays decade after decade,
lip-sounds like a wounded bee.

Science

Conditions are ideal.
The room is soundproof,
the temperature is
cool enough for clear thought.

No expense has been spared.
From the smallest screw
to the crudest fixture
the equipment gleams
in virgin straw.

Still, the vital step eludes him,
stops him like a bombed bridge.
The broken neck of logic
swings above a deep ravine.

Outside the glass laboratory
the ocean hammers at the shore,
each wave riding off
with slivers of hard fact.

The End of the 20th Century

Mr. Smith is not going to Washington

Mr. Smith
is going brown

Disintegrating
into highly-combustible powder

Bleeding nitrates

Murdered by moisture

Mr. Smith is not going to Washington

Mr. Smithi
is dying

In a vault
in Dayton, Ohio

Talking to Robert Mitchum

People invariably get me wrong.
They mistake me
for a deep blue pool
on a hot August day
and dive right in.
They like to make a big splash.
Sure I get tired
but I'll smoke their brands
and nod in all the right places
and make appropriate fishy 'O's
and tut-tut at the debts and doom.
They dig all that
the clichés stinking of truth.
The little man goes home
to the little woman
with a beer belly
and a lighter conscience
as if his sins had just been eaten
by the craggy stranger
whose face he can't quite remember
as he slides into sleep
absolved by its cool surface.
I've an adjustable waveband in my head.
I've yet to find a misery
I can't tune into
chew it up and spit it back
in a neat envelope.
I don't do favours no more
at least not in the active sense
like the old days.
No more guns blazing
downtown in the noon heat
no more roadblocks
and double-crossing dames.

Now I'm more like that wailing wall
smeared with pressures and problems
but still standing.
Sure I get weary
but I don't like to talk about that.

Speed

Dreams are ending everywhere.
Sleepers are anxious
to hurry out
into the loud, ambitious light,
to forget sinister implications,
to leave me here alone
among my crumpled failures,
not worth a spit.

I could go on strike,
demand longer nights,
extended solitude.
But my name carries no weight,
and even as I plead
the bastards are filling
the syringes with tomorrow.

Man Talk

My first wife never made me jelly.
Exceptional in warmth and wit,
miraculous with bread and fish,
I hadn't the heart to tell her
my singular, obsessive wish:

a mould of wobbling scarlet
or transparent green. One ice-cold
spoonful of that prismatic flesh
would have kept me grateful, faithful.

Visiting Rights

The fathers have eaten sour grapes
and the children's teeth are set on edge.

Somehow these are his finest hours,
when the kids swing high on the iron galleon
and the sunlight on their handsome limbs
adds mawkish splendour.

The youngest waves, smiles back
at the old-man bench where he sits
guzzling beer, swallowing gobs of self-pity,
trying hard to quit,

making sense of the uncivil wars,
the various gestures, words and moods,
that have ordained this dazzling judgement day.

The Parkgate Book of the Dead

Away from the scourge of daylight we sit,
transfixed by man-made darkness and uncomplex calm,
in hieroglyphic poses. I am the Jackal, confounded;
you are the Ibis, scarred by your greed for beauty;
and we watch, with other beasts, our lives departing
into the tunnel of the original mystery tour.
We drink to their final journeys,
to the tattered passports of our souls,
and pray that mercy has a sense of humour.

Immured in space, voids of banter
orbit between our elbows,
feeding on photons of strain and silence;
and all that was said before is said again,
the reason and the rubbish, the smashing of promises,
in the cultivated language of destruction,
while we suck each other's bruises
and find each other always on a fallow footing.

Once was the heady green of possibility
sprouting earthly peace.
Once was an open book
loaded with restful heat.
But the seeds of deceit had been planted,
the white pages waiting to burn.

Now, as we relate
our singular falls,
browbeaten Jackal to ageing Ibis,
our eyes become a single eye,
a telescope of pain and longing
scouring earth sea and sky for our cunning.

Now, the screen hollers death in vivid Kodakchrome,
and the corpulent general informs the room
that he, also, doesn't give a rat's butt.
This is how it is, how it must be;
the kerb beyond the door is cracking, oozing gas.
We drink again and breathe it in,
and breathe it in,
and breathe it in…

Classical Music

She turned her grief to the green star,
the only one raining on London.
She picked up the bottle
and smashed the guitar.
The neighbours, perturbed by the music,
screamed – Turn It Down, Turn It Down.
She took off her crown.
She filled up the bath and then
sleepily drowned.
That's Better, they sighed. Classical Music.

Man at a Window

On the canvas of oblong glass
three leaves on the tree.
The sky stops dead above the roof,
The street runs north to south
where I will never go.
This is the terminus,
my exquisite cell.

I paint the walls with sour cream.
I tape the Chinese torture of the tap.
I wear blood-tinted granny-glasses against the light.
Sometimes I roar in the night
and hammer my neighbour's wall.

Every day she passes twice,
my eyes bore holes in hers,
that good girl on a man's bike.

If she were here
I would cradle her like a doll.
My eyes boring holes in hers
I would show her my sharp knife.

Stark Naked Blues

When I wake up
I can't remember who I hurt.
Memory leaves like a paid lover,
an ache clings.
First trains are loudest,
motorways thick with wiseguys
shitting like bluebottles
on dawn's breast.
It's Winter,
Friday the 13th.
No cornflakes in the bowl
and every reason to be blue.
The postman bangs on the door
with a fistful of holiday brochures
and a final notice from the ESB.
He tells me it's really Friday the 14th,
but what the hell.

Once Scratched by Ecstasy

These nights of May,
these blue heralds of summer,
revive a familiar ache.
There's no capsule in the cupboard
strong enough, no affinity
between this pain and diagnosis.
I sit by the raised window
watching Venus burn the hills,
the smoky city stretching to the sea,
and wish I was elsewhere.
With eyes squeezed shut
as fierce as gritted teeth
I feel a cut upon my flesh
from a dead past
which should be long healed.
Instead it throbs and dries
my mouth with a thirst
no liquid on this earth could satisfy.

The Big Picture

One flake of rust
more radiant than sunlight
on the stained-glass of Chartres

One mote of dust
hovering above the peak
of human knowledge

One mutant lark
warbling a wonderful
composition of decay

That's all there is to the picture
we're too frightened to unveil.

A Foreign Christmas

After the dish of the day,
beans and mash and chicken wings,
I take out the sherry and pour
a tall glass for my sick mother.

On the basement steps, in the concrete yard,
the snow is thick and frozen hard,
but the doors, front and back,
are well bolted; the draughts stuffed
with old coats and curtains.

I light the tinsel-curled candle,
plug in the mono portable
and play my mother's favourite songs
from Ireland across the sea.

Over the sweep of the fiddles I hear
the chops and licks of reggae from next door,
and overhead, the thumping of tablas,
the twanging of a lone sitar.

Dream Outlaw

as he drifts towards sleep I begin to awaken

now I'm up
pacing the threadbare carpet
of this temporary room

above me a jet soars away
to some temperate region
while across the street
a gigantic cigarette with glowing neon tip
puffs its electrical way down to the filter
relighting and blooming this hideout
with a fake pink smoke without fire

he doesn't know it
but I've strangled a child
stuffed its little body in a boiler

he doesn't know it
but I hit it harder than I meant
the crack of its skull
like accidentally stomping on a snail

he doesn't know it
but when he wakes up
it is my guilt that will make him suffer.

Lost Children

I was walking too fast
when I lost them.
My mind, a crowded Christmas city,
streamed with tinsel and hype.
The words I should have said
lodged in my throat,
cascaded in my gut.
Too busy with abstract options
I was wrapped-up in the relevance
of the brush I bought that painted me
a dirty shade of grey. I wasn't thinking,
didn't notice the importance of the time.
The warm urgency of their hands in mine
passed cleanly through my flesh,
and when I looked around they were gone.
Ten years were gone and I was walking alone
down an avenue of London Planes
in a Dublin I reached by default.
Each night I dream of them falling into holes,
floating through space, hiding in leafy trees,
running through one door as I come through another.

Mayfly

don't need no mouth
no belly
for my one-day dance

around this green and fecund lake
that's loud with shivering pap
and smells of being born

as I look down from hungry eyes
the hours are pressing
but the sight's a miracle

so I sow my genes and flutter
on this trampoline of water

drawing the sky and the sour lilies
into the frame of a brief life
flying on slowing wings to sundown

From

Looking in at Eden (2001)

Last Night with a Victorian Wardrobe

My flight leaves at ten.
Give me these final hours.
You remind me of someone
I tried to know.
With her swanish neck
in soft black lace,
you retain a semblance
of her perfect grace.
Midnights we shared,
like ours,
a mute impossible love.
She was smooth,
auburn too.
Old-fashioned,
and wooden like you.

Looking in at Eden

1

Walking this street where I live,
with its cracked cement and drying maps of rain,
its slumped casualties of unemployment and booze,
its dirty dogs, junk gardens and mean flowers,
its transient eyes and dingy windows,
with all its poor history of ignorance and want,

sometimes I sense I'm walking
parallel with paradise,
a membrane away from a place
I used to visit long ago.

If I close my eyes
I see sunlight on black rocks,
moonbeams in polished mirrors.
If I seal my ears
I hear sharp explosions of brine,
lurid carousels.

I close my eyes. I seal my ears. I am returned.

2

I wake up free of fingerprints
in an unexplored room at sunrise
excited by the texture of grass
and the taste of fallen apples.
I am back, wading in the stream
near the ash wood where I carved my name.
There is a house, a road,
dependable earth underfoot.

131

Whatever the weather
the faces at the windows
wear the same expressions.
I am a baby bird
fed by their warmth.
Their eyes upon mine

are bloodflecked,
harder than marble.
I believe in permanence,
the angles of the future are trustworthy.
I tie my plans in neat bundles
and place them in the river
that flows in one direction to the sea.

Breeze-light I drop into the long grass.
In the shade of the fruit trees I switch off the world.
Time dies in the playing of light and leaves.
Time is lost forever in the passing of mottled shadows.

Natural Immunity

On a cool August evening
eating air at an open window

watching clouds as they blow
and snag on the city's steel crown,

magnetised by their careless pace,
by the slow retreat of light

at climb of dusk, I ceasefire with myself,
end the tedium of private bickering.

I could be on my knees for years
praying for a peace like this;

I could bleed, thirst and starve
under the thumb of the need

for such a kind release. And here it is,
come without calling,

dropping a fortune at my feet,
demanding neither price nor penance.

Small Ignition

Every morning shortly before seven
the child next door wakes up.
I hear her stirring through the wall.
Her coughs. Her yawns.
The bass thump of her feet against the floor.
Her avid race along the corridor.
Her shrill voice uttering demands
at one, two, three, four
hundred miles an hour.
I name her *small ignition*
spark of an eternal flame.
I press my head against cold stone.
Let her hunger for life
infuse me to the bone.

The Custodian (of Flatworld)

He walks outside to check the fence,
the hundred keys that dangle from his belt
jangling in rhythm with his ex-soldier's stroll.

He snorts at the black faces and the white slobs,
the violated hydrants and the smashed phones.
The language of his tightly-folded arms
says *shoot to kill screw the bastards.*

He runs a strict ship, no messin',
no lip about the mildew,
the water pressure, the faulty wiring.
He nails a list of rules to the front door,
a litany of Nos, tract of a joyless soul.

At night his ears are suctioned to the walls,
taking note of illicit pleasures
and subversive sounds.
The whiskey bottle helps him sleep.
It keeps the twisted image of himself at bay,
under his Superman duvet,
as he lines up tomorrow's troops,
his rubber-soled orderlies of fear.

Watches

They are perfect watches.
Primed for all weather
to coincide with each other.

The oilblack cap on the long face
of lean bone and flapping skin.

The fathead with the fixed scowl
and the certain swagger of the loser.

The night-working soldier
gone stick-like, silent as the grave.

The small man made of soot and rubbish
and an everlasting thirst.

Four watches
in search of a winder

pan the counter
where a hand is wiping
as the hands are wiping
the clock on the wall.
Is it summer already?

Four watches counting
the runners in the 2.15.

Outside, the sun
committing arson on the mountaintop
is but a vertical line
on the stained floor.

Do Not Follow

Do not follow me up the shaky stairs
above the bookies and the boarded bar
to that grimy room where I habitually go.

Where stoned Anna stares at the creased Polaroids
of her confiscated babies tacked above the mantle

where Billy spoons three crystal mole heaps
on a mirror and boils the instruments
in leaky pans on gas of grease and orange

where talk is speedjive of legendary scams
while speakers pour John Cale's viola
across a floor of knickers hard with semen.

Where would you park yourself in there,
your rustic eyes, your healthy skin?
Go home. Alone, I plead to enter.

Nikitara Street

I leave him twisted,
broiled between the sheets,
near-demented from raw Raki,
on the blind side of the moon.
The island of Rhodes is burning.
Skips full of rotting vegetables
wobble and steam. Colours sweat.
Gold dust streams down
Nikitara Street.
Through a gap in a sagging plank
I watch a woman sweep
a marble stair,
and I envy the muscle,
the tender purpose
that animates her broom.
I walk as one abandoned,
one whose dreams are ruined.
The lush Akiki trees,
the brash Piaggio scooters,
the scarlet leaves
are negatives.
My lover's darkness
follows me, like some shifty
sneaky pick-up artist,
around the holy walls
of the Avenue of Martyrs,
down to the harbour
where I sit, feet in the water.
The view is luminous.
I should be screaming
bravo beauty,
but my heart is bluer
than the skin of the Aegean.

A Western Dirge

On a freak blue February afternoon
West Nine by the canal
With bags at my feet
And sweat on my back
I had to look down at my shoes
I was drowning in your eyes
My hand shook as it shook yours
My fingers craving informality
My skin wanting to hold on
But a curtain fell
And when I crossed the road
It was like crossing a wild wide river
In a bullet-hole canoe

I vanished into a tacky bar
Drank until my hands and heart
Stopped shaking
Over and over the jukebox played
A Western dirge

Railroad steamboat river and canal
Yonder comes a sucker and he's got my gal

A song of thwarted love
The way I felt
A song of jealousy
Malicious fate
A song of violence and flight

A flight was waiting to take me away
To take me back to my present life
But I wanted to be like the men at the bar
To live here in this godforsaken twilight
And be going nowhere

At the Tomb of the Unknown Father

I built my nest in you.
You grew on me
a second skin
as apt and cosy as my own.
I was safe
in the knowledge of your eyes.
When the stars were blotted out,
when the sea-line drowned the jetty
and waves rolled down our street
I was sure of my guns,
held in the grip of your solid voice,
gripped in the vice of your promises.
Where have you gone, my father?
To whom do you cling
when the lights go out
now that I who loved you
am nothing but a junction
you thoughtlessly departed?

Haunted

That dress I wore
the night you beat me
I cannot wear it anymore.

It hangs in my wardrobe,
the bloodstains blending
with the pattern,
like the skin of some exotic
eviscerated animal.

I want to cleanse its line
and texture from my mind,
to drown it,
or incinerate its legacy.

What can I do?
If I give it to charity
the innocent will suffer.
If I cast it in the river
the fish will surely die.
If I burn it, surely the wind
will blind me with smoke.

That Place You Go

That place you go,
don't go there anymore.
Its wide, hypnotic door will sting,
then spin you like a webbed fly.
It is a world unto its two-faced self,
with a miniature sun
whose daubed black smile
will encourage your mouth to run,
to spill your bland beans,
your cheap shots,
your overkill.

That place you go,
don't go there anymore.
Its amiable gloom
will rob you of your memories.
You'll wind up playing
to an audience of one,
self-snared into believing
there are hosts of allies in the dark,
when every self-respecting soul
is longtime gone.

The Real World

i'm nine years old
glued to the Savoy screen
where a desert
courtesy of 20th Century Fox
shimmers and blinds

alone and ragged
a figure looms into view
like a Christian martyr
with a halo of vultures

and he shrieks
as he stumbles
upon the disembowelled corpse
of the horse
he thought he'd left
so far behind

The Silver Screen

Spotlit in crimson and lavendar
Fred Bridgeman, the tropical organist, sets.
Sliced down the middle waves
the Red Sea curtains part.
Crescendo of muted strings,
the golden lion roars.
A cloudburst of dazzle
hushes the mouths
of the chewing multitudes.
Technicolour spreads
over craned necks
and flickers in widening eyes.

Later, down the marble steps
excited children roll,
shooting with stiff fingers,
cocking triggers with tongues.
By monochrome windows
in the rain their elders sit
and dream of Monroe's bosom
and her bombshell lips.

Last Dance
i.m. Bernadette Murphy

Partner me, one final time,
before your saviour takes you home.
Let's treat the neighbours
to a twist extravaganza
as lurid as a *Photoplay* or *Reveille;*
I'll be Rock Hudson and Rosanno Brazzi,
Troy Donohue and Mario Lanza.
Let's rock once more around the block,
Mount Pleasant Avenue, Friar's Walk,
South Summerhill and Douglas Street.
I'll dance the cold from your dead feet.

I know you're tired now and I must let you go,
let you finger-click into the sun
to the happy strings of Hadjidakis.
Pale blonde, unlikely sister of the Mediterranean,
your geography enchanted me,
Rimini, Capri, Sorrento, Napoli;
we settled for drizzly Winter nights
in the Woodbine light
of the Colosseum picture house.
When we played Old Maid
in the gardens of Crosshaven
how could I have known
you were born to lose?
You held your cards close to the chest,
a woman in love with your secrets,
responding cryptically through twinkling eyes,
plush curtains pulled on your innermost thoughts.

The greatest astronomer on earth
can't spot you now.
So how can I, with feeble eye,
achieve a staring
grave enough to picture you.
Cold-storaged in a square of field,
gone from the torment, the hustling game,
losing your handsome smile to the worms
and your name to the Irish rain.